C L A S S I C
StoryTellers

JACK LONDON

Mitchell Lane
PUBLISHERS

P.O. Box 196
Hockessin, Delaware 19707

Titles in the Series

C L A S S I C
StoryTellers

JACK LONDON

by John Bankston

Copyright © 2005 by Mitchell Lane Publishers, Inc. All rights reserved. No part of this book may be reproduced without written permission from the publisher. Printed and bound in the United States of America.

Printing   1   2   3   4   5   6   7   8
    Library of Congress Cataloging-in-Publication Data
Bankston, John, 1974-
        Jack London / John Bankston.
            p. cm. — (Classic storytellers)
        Includes bibliographical references (p.) and index.
        Contents: Dangerous journey—Hard times—Workers of the world—Literary gold—Money and love.
        ISBN 1-58415-263-X (lib. bdg.)
        1. London, Jack, 1876-1916—Juvenile literature. 2. Authors, America—20th century—Biography—Juvenile literature. [1. London, Jack, 1876-1916. 2. Authors, American. 3. Authorship.] I. Title. II. Series.
        PS3523.046Z6113 2004
        813'.52—dc22
                                                                    2003024131

ABOUT THE AUTHOR: Born in Boston, Massachusetts, John Bankston has written over three dozen biographies for young adults profiling scientists like Jonas Salk and Alexander Fleming, celebrities like Mandy Moore and Alicia Keys, great achievers like Alfred Nobel, and master musicians like Mozart. He worked in Los Angeles, California as a producer, screenwriter and actor. Currrently he is in preproduction on *Dancing at the Edge*, a semi-autobiographical film he hopes to film in Portland, Oregon. Last year he completed his first young adult novel, *18 to Look Younger.*

PHOTO CREDITS: Cover, pp. 1, 3, 6 Getty Images; p. 8 Library of Congress; p. 20 Barbara Marvis; pp. 12, 30, 35, 38 The Bancroft Library, University of California

PUBLISHER'S NOTE: This story is based on the author's extensive research, which he believes to be accurate. Documentation of such research is contained on page 46.

The internet sites referenced herein were active as of the publication date. Due to the fleeting nature of some web sites, we cannot guarantee they will all be active when you are reading this book.

Contents

JACK LONDON
by John Bankston

*For Your Information

A portrait of Jack London taken in 1905, two years after he wrote Call of the Wild.

Chapter 1

A DANGEROUS JOURNEY

Churning and crashing along the jagged rocks, the Fifty Mile River swept through the Yukon Territory like a flume ride at an amusement park. Its fury was real, its dangers obvious. When Jack London climbed into a boat he'd constructed after chopping down some trees, riding the river seemed foolhardy. Yet there was no turning around, no going home for Jack. Instead, he shouted instructions to the other men in his boat. The water's rage often drowned out his voice.

"The water, though swift, had a slick oily appearance until we dashed into the very jaws of the Box [Rapids], where it instantly took on the appearance of chaos broken loose,"[1] he would later write in the article "Through the Rapids on the Way to Klondike."

He called his crude boat the *Yukon Belle*. Although she creaked and leaked, she held the men's supplies. Their survival in the Yukon's unforgiving conditions depended on keeping her afloat.

Jack was in Alaska for the same reason as more than 100,000 other men. He had gold fever. Gold fever swept along the western coast of the United States during the early summer of 1897. It was

Gold prospectors moving to a new gold field. This photograph was taken around 1888 just after gold fever started to sweep the United States. With long odds and poor conditions, many men sold all their possessions for the chance to strike it rich.

just as contagious as the common cold, as dangerous as the bubonic plague. All across the country, men were out of work. The promise of riches arrived after a single prospector panned a few ounces from a river in the Yukon Territory. Although striking it rich was as likely as winning the lottery, men sold everything they had and spent immense sums of money to travel north to Alaska.

Jack was one of them. In a later book, he described the final push to the mining camp as the river rapidly began to freeze around the *Yukon Belle*. "Their speed began to diminish and cakes of ice to up-end and crash and smash about them....Then all movement ceased....Once again it started, running swiftly and savagely with a great grinding. Then they saw lights ashore and when abreast, gravity and the Yukon surrendered, and the river ceased for six months."[2]

Jack and his companions were lucky. They found an abandoned cabin formerly used by a fur trader. During a half year of winter, Jack suffered disease and hunger. When the brutal cold ended, Jack realized he was nearly out of money, and too sick to mine. He returned home with a few souvenir flecks of gold for his efforts.

He also brought back something much more valuable.

Jack brought back experience. For years he'd tried to make a living as a writer. He'd grown up poor, abandoned by his father even before he was born. He'd been raised by a disabled Civil War veteran who married his mother, a woman given to violent and unpredictable mood swings. At 14, he dropped out of school to support the family, working in factories and on ships. He attended college for just a semester before dropping out because he felt too confined and impatient.

Chapter 1 A DANGEROUS JOURNEY

Before his trip to Alaska, every story he submitted was re-jected. Afterwards he mined the experience as certainly as he'd planned to mine for gold. The wealth of his stories lasted much longer than gold ever would. Over the course of his brief lifetime, he authored more than four dozen novels and even more short stories. He became a best-selling author in the United States. Today he is one of the most widely read writers of all time. Jack London wrote about the life he lived.

It was the life of a classic storyteller.

FYInfo

GOLD FEVER

The American West was settled by many men who dreamed of finding gold. Yet no place was as forbidding and dangerous for treasure seekers as the Klondike, where temperatures could fall to as low as 70 degrees below zero. When George Carmack filled an empty shotgun shell with gold dust he had uncovered in Rabbit Creek in 1896, it became much more explosive than gunpowder. Word of his discovery traveled south the following year. By mid-summer of 1897, an exodus was underway. Filled with images of untold wealth, gold-seekers cashed in their life savings and packed their bags. The northern migration of more than 100,000 men began. Quite a few would find death, not riches.

Located in Canada's Yukon Territory, the Klondike was bordered by the Rocky Mountains. The only way to avoid the treacherous range was through Alaska. After traversing the steep Chilkoot Pass, a nearly vertical trail littered with the rotting corpses of abandoned horses, the travelers had to build their own boats. Then their overwater journey crossed five lakes and rapids-filled rivers like Fifty Mile.

Their goal was to arrive at Dawson. A once sleepy town hard up

A Gold Prospector

against the Yukon River, its population boomed overnight. Made up of tents and cheap buildings, the town offered overpriced food, liquor and seedy entertainment. Ten million dollars in gold was extracted from the Klondike but over 60 million dollars was spent in Dawson.

Despite the risks and hardships, prospectors kept coming. They were fed by stories brought back by writers like James S. Easby-Smith, who described one treasure-laden ship as holding "more than a million dollars worth of virgin gold in dust, flakes and nuggets, wrapped in blankets, tied up in canvas bags and the skins of animals and poured into bottles and cans."[1]

Jack London hoped to get just a portion of that treasure.

John London, Jack's stepfather, lost one of his lungs while serving as a soldier in the Civil War. John treated Jack as if he was his son by birth. That included giving him the last name by which he would become famous.

Chapter 2

HARD TIMES

When Jack London was fourteen, he began supporting his family by working in Oakland's Hickmott's Canning Factory. At an age when most kids are learning at school or playing games with friends, Jack was counting cans, surrounded by the stink of fish guts.

"I was up and at work at six in the morning....I worked every night till ten, eleven, and twelve o'clock," he later wrote to his friend Mabel Applegarth. "My wages were small, but I worked such long hours that I sometimes made as high as fifty dollars a month. I turned every cent over [to my mother]. My body and soul were starved when I was a child."[1]

His mother was hardly appreciative of her son's agony.

Flora London was the youngest child in the wealthy Marshall Wellman household in Massillon,

Chapter 2   HARD TIMES

Ohio. Her father made his money buying and selling wheat. He made sure his children had every luxury. Still, her childhood was marked by early troubles. When she was 12 years old, Flora caught typhoid fever. The disease stunted her growth and caused her hair to fall out. She'd spend the rest of her life in a wig and children's shoes, overcome by violent and unpredictable moods.

Her adulthood was just as wild and reckless. At 25, she left her home's security for the untamed west. After a brief stop in Seattle, she arrived in San Francisco, California in the 1870s. San Francisco was a boomtown, fed by the dreamers of the Gold Rush that began in 1849 and the vagabonds and businessmen who followed. Sometimes it seemed like houses were built overnight. Bankers rubbed elbows with adventure seekers. Saloons, gambling houses and brothels were ready to free men of their money, while occultists and practitioners of bizarre religions fed on those with less fortune.

It was a town where an astrologer named William Chaney earned a living reading the stars and predicting the future. Flora moved in with Chaney in 1874. The arrangement lasted until Flora became pregnant. Chaney didn't want to take care of a child and quickly left. Born John Griffith Chaney on January 12, 1876 (but called Jack by nearly everyone), the boy would not know his biological father for years. Soon after giving birth, Flora met John London, a middle-aged Civil War veteran with a young daughter named Eliza. The couple was married in September and John London did everything he could to treat Jack as if the boy was his son by birth. That included giving him the last name by which he would become famous.

Jack saw John London as a shining light. Unfortunately, the war had cost London a lung and weakened him. He was no match for Flora's temper. Her moods determined nearly every decision the family made. She demanded that her new husband beat Jack regularly for the slightest infraction.

Flora paid little attention to her son. The first year of his life, he barely saw his mother. The job of nursing him and taking care of him fell to an African American woman named Virginia Prentiss. Called Mammie Jennie by Jack, she'd lost a baby in childbirth shortly before. Besides Mammie, Eliza also treated him more like her child than his mother did.

Before he was six, Jack caught diphtheria. So did Eliza. On a doctor's advice, the family left San Francisco and moved across the bay for much quieter and still-rural Oakland. Although the health of Jack and Eliza motivated that move, Flora's unending ambitions drove the rest. There was never enough money to satisfy her. Each triumph demanded another. The family moved from one farm to the next. By the mid-1880s, John London owned nearly 100 acres.

All too soon, Jack watched his family fall apart. With his stepfather struggling to pay bills, the family took in a boarder named J.H. Shepard. The former army captain was in his 40s, but his attentions soon wandered to 16-year-old Eliza. When the couple eloped and left the London household, Jack was devastated.

His mother gave him little comfort. She was too consumed with her own emptiness to worry about her son's. Young Jack was secretly pleased when the family's latest financial setback forced a return to Oakland. Not only was the city more interesting, their new home was just a few short blocks from where Eliza and her husband lived with his three children.

Chapter 2 HARD TIMES

Attending Garfield Elementary School, Jack was bothered by bullies. He was slight for his age, and looked vulnerable. But, he held his own in every fight. Maybe his toughness was developed by farm work, or from enduring battles at home. Outside of school, life got worse. John London was unable to pay for their house. The family moved to a teeming slum in West Oakland, an area filled with recent immigrants, primarily from Asia. This only fueled the racist speeches of his mother. Other conflicts aside, Jack agreed with his mother's belief in the superiority of the white race.

"My mother had theories," he'd later write in his memoir, *John Barleycorn*. "First she steadfastedly maintained that brunettes and all the tribe of dark-eyed humans were deceitful. Needless to say she was a blonde."[2]

After their move, Jack attended Cole Grammar School. Keeping up with his studies was nearly impossible. When his stepfather was badly hurt at the Oakland railroad yards, he was unable to work. At the age of 14, Jack had just graduated from Cole. Now he would have to take over the job of supporting the family.

Working 12-hour shifts at the canning factory left little time for anything but dreams. He couldn't even save money. All summer he worked to buy an eight-dollar skiff, a tiny rowboat. "In the fall I had five dollars as a result of absolutely doing without all pleasure," he wrote in a letter to his friend Mabel Applegarth. "My mother came to the machine where I worked and asked for it. I could have killed myself that night. After a year of hell, to have that pitiful—to be robbed of that petty joy."[3]

Despite that disappointment, Jack's days of doing without pleasure were about to end. He discovered the dubious happiness of drinking.

"I was in the flower of my adolescence, a thrill with romance and adventure, dreaming of wild life in the wild-man world," he recalled in *John Barleycorn*. "Little I guessed how all the warp and woof of that man-world was entangled with alcohol."[4]

He began frequenting the rough bars around the docks, places where getting served liquor meant only having the quarter for a shot of whiskey. His long days of labor found some relief in casual camaraderie and strong drink. Still, Jack couldn't find the refuge he needed. Instead, he sought out another, less damaging escape. That was books.

"I read everything," he'd later write. "I read mornings, afternoons and nights. I read in bed. I read at the table. I read as I walked to and from school, and I read at recess while the other boys were playing."[5]

Lying under a shade tree with a book during a hot farm summer had been just a pleasurable pastime as a child. At 14, books became more significant. Inside the Oakland Library, Jack London found a guide and a champion. The librarian, Ina Coolbrith, helped him locate everything from adventure stories to the works of one of America's best known short story writers, Washington Irving.

Reading gave Jack direction.

He realized there were better ways to earn a living than working in a factory. The stench and noise were not the worst part. It was looking down the aisles at men two or three times his age, whose lives seemed like a prison of monotonous work and misery.

Jack found a solution to his problem at the bar. It didn't come out of the mouth of a bottle. It came out of the mouths of the men who drank there. They told stories of adventure and fortune, stories about working on the ocean and in the harbors. Jack decided to be an oyster pirate.

Oyster piracy was a huge business. Under the cover of night, and piloting a quiet boat, bandits would break into private oyster traps. In a single night, a skilled oyster thief could make 50 dollars. This was as much as Jack made in a month at canning. But to make this kind of money, Jack first had to spend money. He needed a boat. A man named French Frank was selling a suitable one, but his asking price was 300 dollars. It might as well have been three million. Jack London didn't have it, and his family sure didn't have it. There was only one person who might have it.

Mammie Jennie was a heck of a saver—and a savior. She agreed to loan him the cash. That same day his pockets were heavy with her gold coins, as he raced to the docks. He sealed the deal with Frank at the First and Last Chance Saloon.

For three months, Jack lived a life of adventure. By stealing oysters he risked going to jail. Commanding a crew of men twice his age he risked even more. He survived it all. He even had a girlfriend, a 16-year-old named Mamie who lived with her sister Tess on board the boat. He almost earned more than he could spend. He took care of his family, and blew the rest on liquor and fun.

Three months later, his boat was heavily damaged by fire. A stark choice presented itself. He could return to the drudgery of factory work, or apply what he'd already learned in a new career. It was an easy decision. Just a short time after he'd made a living as a thief, Jack was back on the water. This time he worked for the Fish Patrol, arresting men he'd once called his friends.

FYInfo

INA COOLBRITH

Ina Coolbrith, born in Illinois in 1841, shared more than a love of books with Jack London. Like Jack, Ina was largely self-educated after coming west to California when she was 10. Although she received some education in Los Angeles, in the 1850s it was a sleepy small town. The future careers of young women weren't considered.

Ina published several poems during her early teens. After a brief and unhappy marriage when she was 17, she moved to San Francisco. She refused to let either her lack of formal education or her gender hold her back. Because she was so well-read and already had some of her poetry published, she became friends with up-and-coming young writers such as Mark Twain and Bret Harte. Harte had founded the literary magazine *Overland Monthly* and thought she'd be the perfect co-editor.

She took the job and showed a talent for identifying promising young writers and championing their work in the pages of the magazine. When Harte moved back east to capitalize on his fame as a writer, Ina chose to stay behind even though she would have advanced her career if she had

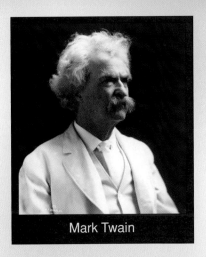

Mark Twain

done the same thing. She felt responsible for supporting several family members.

She became a librarian at the Oakland Library in 1874 and spent nearly two decades there. She influenced many young people besides Jack, spending so much time with them that her own work suffered. Ina's three thin volumes of poetry were all she published. Yet the writers she discovered and encouraged made her contributions to late 19th century literature as valuable as any author's. In 1915, the governor and legislature of California named her the state's poet laureate. She died in 1928. Not long afterward the California Assembly named a 7,900-foot-high peak as Mt. Ina Coolbrith.

A view of the San Francisco Bay and the Golden Gate Bridge. Jack's near drowning in the Carquinez Straits at the northern end of San Francisco Bay forced him to reconsider the direction his life was taking.

Chapter 3

WORKERS OF THE WORLD

Jack London was drunk again. Stumbling, he moved along the edge of the sloop he was planning to turn into his makeshift bed. Suddenly he pitched over the side. He plunged into the chilly Carquinez Straits at the northern end of San Francisco Bay. Jack struggled against the powerful currents. Despite his efforts, the lights of land quickly receded into the background.

And then Jack decided to give up. The warm alcohol and cold water were a deadly combination. He let himself go and let the straits do their job. Even as he prepared to die, something happened. His will to live returned. He pushed his muscles, giving all he had, but it wasn't enough. His muscles began to cramp from the effects of being immersed in cold water for several hours. He couldn't hold out much longer. In the nick of time, a fisherman spotted him and pulled him to safety. The future writer resolved to focus.

He'd been employed with the Fish Patrol. Arresting those he'd once drunk with was hard enough. Yet by 1892 his life in Oakland seemed like a dark and never-ending tunnel. He needed to escape.

The sea had almost killed Jack. Now it gave him a way out of his dilemma. He took a job on the *Sophia Sutherland*, a sealer bound for Japan. Ships such as the *Sophia Sutherland* set sail with one goal: filling the hull with as many seal skins as they could carry. It was brutal work, but it would give him a nine-month reprieve from the demands of his mother.

Three years shy of his 17th birthday, Jack got the job because of his well-earned reputation. He was known as a bit of a brawler and a hard drinker, but also as a teenager unafraid of hard work. On board the ship, he'd prove it. He shared a cabin with some of the toughest men he'd seen.

In his book *The Sea Wolf*, he described them: "The men, like butchers plying their trade, naked and red of arm and hand, hard at work with ripping and flensing-knives, removing the skins from the pretty sea-creatures they had killed."[1]

Returning home after nine arduous months, he realized that he had less money saved than he'd hoped. Soon he'd be back at work, toiling ten-hour shifts inside a jute factory for a dollar a day. His wages were the same, despite his increased strength and stamina. Hard work seemed to have little reward.

This time his mother renewed Jack's focus. She pointed out a writing contest in the *San Francisco Morning Call* for writers under the age of 22 and encouraged him to enter. He did, completing the first draft of a 4,000-word essay in a single sleepless night. He spent several more days whittling it down to the required 2,000-word maximum.

"Each mighty sea, all phosphorescent and glowing with the tiny lights of the myriad animalcule, threatened to overwhelm us with a deluge of fire," Jack's story began. "Higher and higher, thinner and thinner, the crest grew as it began to curve and overtop preparatory to breaking...."[2]

Wordy and rambling, his effort still impressed the contest judges as they plowed through submissions. They gave Jack first prize. The 25-dollar award wasn't as important to Jack as the knowledge that he was now a professional writer.

His next check for writing was a long way away. He returned to the factory. Now the labor seemed so much harder. Pouring his thoughts onto paper was more fulfilling, if not better paying. A short time after winning the contest, Jack quit his job. His timing could not have been worse. The United States was in the middle of its first modern depression. Factories and farms shed workers left and right. Across the nation, millions of people were out of work. Every job opening brought a flood of qualified applicants.

In response, various worker movements gained support during this period. Labor unions began striking, and socialists demanded equal shares of the country's wealth. The writings of communist philosopher Karl Marx gained an audience. Marx railed against capitalism, the system on which the U.S. economy was based.

Jack soon embraced the idea that capitalism with its boom and bust cycles was inherently evil. He drew inspiration from writer Friedrich Nietzsche, whose philosophy of the Superman meshed with Jack's belief that some men are created superior.

In 1894, Jack began to consider the needs of unemployed workers. After all, he was one of them. Across the country, in Flora London's birthplace of Massillon, Ohio, a man named Jacob Coxey commanded thousands of unemployed workers. He planned to lead a march to Washington, D.C. As an organized "army," they would demand government jobs, like road construction and building repair. In California, one of Coxey's supporters, Charles T. Kelly, convinced West Coast railroad lines to donate space in boxcars so the men could make the cross-country trip. The railroads agreed. Their transportation offer helped motivate men like Jack London to join up. After all, he had nothing to lose.

Jack arrived late and missed traveling with the main group. He hitched a series of illegal rides on trains before catching up. When the group arrived in Des Moines, Iowa, the train rides stopped. The men were ready to give up. Jack came to the rescue. He organized the workers and they began building crude rafts. Traveling from the Des Moines River to the Mississippi, and then up the Ohio River, the group managed to reach Wheeling, West Virginia. A relatively brief land march took them to the nation's capital.

By then weather and hardship had whittled the "army of thousands" to a few hundred tired and hungry men. Coxey's attempt to present his petitions for work got him arrested for trespassing. The difficult journey did little for most of its participants. For Jack, it gave him the seed of an idea. A decade later, his book *The Road* would describe the experience. It would also inspire numerous writers of similar works, such as Jack Kerouac in his *On the Road*.

After the debacle in the nation's capital, Jack fled to New York City. He stayed until the urban spectacle of the poor and struggling became too much to bear. Making his way to upstate New York, neither lack of cash nor prospects kept him from enjoying the majesty of Niagara Falls. The pleasure was short lived. A police officer questioned Jack about where he lived. Unable to prove a permanent residence, Jack was arrested for vagrancy. Despite his arguments, the judge didn't believe him any more than the cop had. Jack London was sentenced to 30 days of hard labor.

Jail was a tough haul. Jack endured a place far worse than prisons today. Still, he managed to again prove his toughness, fighting with the hardest inmates until he became a hall man—one of those in charge of the other prisoners.

Making his way home, Jack London felt like a total failure. A future of drudge jobs seemed like another excuse to try drowning. Without an education there seemed to be few other options. Jack realized he needed to finish high school. In the 1890s, he couldn't just take a test and get a diploma. If he wanted to graduate from high school, he'd have to go back and become a student again. Jack decided to give it a try.

Returning to high school was embarrassing. Jack, now 19, was entering the ninth grade. He stood out among students who were five or six years younger. Jack's after-school job as a janitor didn't help his ego as he cleaned up after the same kids he'd sat beside during the day.

"My sister helped me, too; and I was not above mowing anybody's lawn or taking up and beating carpets when I had half a day to spare," he later wrote. "I was working to get away from work, and I buckled down to it with the grim realization of the paradox."[3]

Somehow, Jack endured.

25

Chapter **3** WORKERS OF THE WORLD

Again, he found solace in the Oakland Public Library. He began reading *The Communist Manifesto* by Karl Marx. According to Marx, all human history consists of continuous clashes between exploiters and the people they exploit for their own selfish gain. Jack embraced Marx's philosophy. He joined the Henry Clay Debating Society as one of its few members who hadn't attended college. He registered with the Socialist Labor Party. And he began speaking about his beliefs, in meetings with the society and on the public street corners of Oakland.

Between school and politics, Jack still found time for a social life. He'd had brief involvements with women before, from girls and woman who lived near the wharfs to a well-described "Sweet Sixteen" romance which many historians believe was a total fiction.

Mabel Applegarth was quite real. Twenty-one years old and a student at the University of California at Berkeley, she was Jack London's first true love. She also represented a world Jack had never seen before.

Mabel came from an upper-middle-class family, with an attractive, well-cared-for home. Yet despite his worn clothes and rough exterior, Mabel's parents liked Jack as much as she did. Although he and Mabel began dating, he realized their relationship could go no further so long as he was poor. In his heart, Jack wanted to marry Mabel. He began to dream about being a successful writer, the most successful in the world—a writer who could provide Mabel with a lifestyle even better than the one she'd grown up with.

His dreams of riches contrasted with his speeches. Preaching about the evils of capitalism on local streets, the "Boy Socialist of Oakland," as some newspapers called him, was getting quite a reputation. When he protested a city law forbidding speaking to groups on public streets, Jack was arrested. During his jury trial, the high school student made an impassioned argument against his arrest and the law.

When Jack won the case, newspapers across the country reported the decision. The story didn't sit well with his fellow debaters or the high school administration. Most Henry Clay members stopped inviting him to their homes. He was also kicked out of school when parents complained. They were worried that Jack might influence younger students to support socialism.

With his high school diploma dreams destroyed after nearly two years of struggle, Jack decided to go straight to college. If he passed the entrance exam at the University of California, he would be admitted despite his interrupted education. Jack began studying non-stop for the test. Although he continued to see Mabel, he soon met another woman who would have a much greater influence on his life.

Her name was Bess Maddern, and she was engaged to Henry Clay member Fred Jacobs. She was also a math teacher. She began to help Jack with his test preparations. Their hard work paid off. He passed the exams and was able to attend the prestigious college in the fall of 1896. Right away Jack's self-taught ways and rough experiences clashed with the education at Berkeley.

Soon Jack decided college was bad idea. He was too impatient. His time at Berkeley wasn't a complete waste. He focused on three things: learning to box, getting published, and finding his real father.

Boxing came naturally to the street-taught fighter, but he suffered a few hard blows before he grasped the sport's fundamentals. Jack had less success getting published. Now on a one thousand word a day regimen, he began sending out stories regularly to various magazines.

He worked as a writer the same way he had at the factory and on the boats. He worked when he was sick, tired, or hung over. He put a blue-collar work ethic into a white-collar profession. His hard work didn't pay off right away. Jack got nothing for his trouble but rejection letters. The publishers weren't interested in the stories he wrote. Still he didn't give up.

His search for his father was the most frustrating of all his quests. In the office of the *San Francisco Chronicle*, Jack scoured the back issues. In an article dated June 4, 1875, he read a story entitled "A Discarded Wife." He read about the astrologer W. H. Chaney and his wife, Flora. According to the article, when Chaney learned she was pregnant, "He told her that she had better destroy her unborn babe. This she indignantly declined to do."[4] Because of her refusal, Chaney abandoned her. Flora tried to commit suicide by shooting herself. She suffered only a flesh wound and friends quickly disarmed her.

Jack learned that Chaney was in Chicago. He wrote to Chaney, who responded to Jack's letters with denials. He swore he was not his father, although he admitted knowing Flora. Jack didn't believe him. He saw the resemblance in the photo accompanying the article. It was like looking at himself in another 30 years.

By 1897, Jack was about to make another life-changing decision. It was a choice that would almost kill him. It would also give him the kind of material every aspiring writer dreams of.

FYInfo

FRIEDRICH NIETZSCHE

Looking around him, Jack London saw nothing but conflict. He saw the divisions between rich and poor, between the weak and the strong. He saw struggle. And he saw some men rise to the top, regardless of family advantages or connections. This curiosity attracted Jack to the writings of Friedrich Nietzsche.

Born in 1844 as the son of a Lutheran minister, Nietzsche avoided the family's religious tradition. He was a brilliant student who studied philosophy and became a university professor at the age of 24. He played classical music, such as the works of Richard Wagner and Frédéric Chopin. Before he was 30, in 1872, Nietzsche published his first significant book, *The Birth of Tragedy*. This book and the works that followed displayed a philosophy opposed to the beliefs of his time. He suffered from ill health for much of his adult life, and went insane in 1890. He died in 1900.

Nietzsche's rebellion fascinated Jack London. So too did the philosopher's ideas that idealism is false and religion a crutch. Nietzsche attacked the Christian religion, saying in one of his books that "God is dead." Raised by a racist mother, Jack believed in the superiority of the white race and Anglo Saxons in

Friedrich Nietzsche

particular. He believed incorrectly that Nietzsche shared this belief.

It was Nietzsche, rather than comic book writers, who was responsible for the creation of "Superman." In his philosophy, traditional religion and other influences encouraged what he called a "slave morality" that kept people from fully realizing their potential. A few people, however, could rise above these restrictions and become an *Ubermensch*, a term that can be translated as "superman," "overman," or "higher man." According to Nietzsche, such an individual is superior to the average person and can overcome any obstacles. Jack was certain he was such a man. He made the philosopher's system his own, as he chose to live dangerously and was comfortable with his own egoism.

Even though Jack never found gold, his adventures in the Yukon Territory were more valuable. He wrote about those adventures and the wealth of his stories lasted much longer than gold ever would.

Chapter 4

LITERARY GOLD

"It was like taking an anesthetic. Freezing was not as bad as people thought. There were lots worse ways to die."[1] So went the last thoughts of the narrator in "To Build a Fire," Jack London's short story about a man's slow battle against frostbite and hypothermia. It has become one of the most widely read short stories in history.

And Jack London almost didn't live long enough to write it.

"Write what you know." It's the advice given by many teachers. Jack's experiences soon gave him enough material to become a professional.

When George Carmack's discovery of gold in Canada's Yukon Territory was reported in the United States, it sparked the dreams of thousands of men. Despite the long odds and horrible conditions, many of them sold all they had to finance the exploration. After completing the nearly 2,000-mile journey, they could stake a claim—getting the right to search for gold in a small area. Panning a river could produce enough gold to change a man's life. The risks seemed inconsequential.

Jack London was working in an industrial laundry with few prospects when he learned of Carmack's discovery. There was no way he could afford to buy the equipment he needed and make the trip. He quickly found an eager champion. Eliza's husband, Captain Shepard, was fascinated by the stories from the Yukon. Terminally ill, he wanted one last shot at the kind of adventure he'd known in the military. Jack was reluctant. As a partner on the trip, Shepard would be little more than a burden. He was past 60 and suffered from a heart condition.

Shepard was insistent. Since Jack needed his money to finance the trip, he agreed. The two men joined the long lines of similar dreamers buying supplies, stocking everything from a year's worth of canned food to fur-lined gloves and parkas. Their gear alone weighed a ton.

In the end, agreeing to let the Captain come worked out. Two days after landing at Juneau, the gateway to the Yukon, Shepard turned around and went home. Jack proceeded by himself. Reaching the Yukon meant crossing high mountain passes, forging violent rivers and following treacherous paths. Although Jack left in July, winter had already set in before he could cover the final 75 miles to the mining town of Dawson.

Jack spent the long winter stranded with several other gold-seekers in an abandoned cabin. Beneath the unrelenting brightness of winter sun and snow, Jack scribbled in his diary, read, and earned a reputation as a great storyteller. By the time winter concluded in mid-May, Jack was sick from scurvy. The disease, caused by a lack of vegetables and fruits, turned his skin gray and gave him horrible dental problems. The illness and his lack of money forced him to give up his gold ambitions. Instead, he spent a few weeks in Dawson. The town was expensive and lawless, hardly the ideal location for an impoverished writer.

Returning home was only slightly less dangerous. For a time, Jack and a few others were able to drift lazily down the Yukon River, letting the current do the work. Attacks by hordes of mosquitoes and the eventual need to trek overland kept the journey from being a pleasure cruise. Jack's biting sense that once again he'd failed was as bad as the mosquitoes.

Oakland offered little joy when Jack returned. His stepfather had died while he was away. His mother needed his support more than ever before. He took up the familiar difficult jobs, but mainly he wrote. Night and day he turned his experiences in Alaska into stories.

His failure in the Klondike damaged Jack London in ways he'd rarely admit. The change bled into his work. His stories were as hard-edged as before, and even more realistic. Yet now they had a sensitivity, a depth that the schoolboy yarns he'd submitted the year before lacked.

Despite the improvement in his ability, Jack London did not find immediate success. The editor of *The San Francisco Bulletin* rejected Jack's story proposals with the depressing opinion that "interest in Alaska has subsided to an amazing degree."[2] Jack refused to give up. He continued to write and submit. Finally the young adult magazine *Black Cat* offered him $50 if he'd trim a story he'd submitted by 50 percent. Jack quickly did so.

The check barely covered Jack's time and materials. Worse, he'd been offered a job at the post office, a position that promised stability. This time it was his mother who saved him. She urged Jack to continue writing. She knew he'd make it if he stuck with it.

She was right.

Just half a year after he pulled into Oakland Harbor, *The Overland Monthly* accepted one of his stories, "To the Man on Trail." It was the most respected magazine on the West Coast. The connection surely helped Jack get his career in a new direction.

Jack followed the sale with "The White Silence," which *The Overland Monthly* bought as well. He'd acquired an essential ability for a professional writer. He knew what editors and publishers wanted. And he gave it to them. He fashioned rough-hewn adventures that were distinct from the work of writers who spent most of their time behind a desk. Jack London had lived much of the life he described. It showed.

Soon Jack sold "An Odyssey of the North" to New York City-based *The Atlantic Monthly*. The magazine's $120 payment was far less important than the respect the sale gave him. One result was that Jack quickly attracted the attention of publisher Houghton Mifflin, which brought out a collection of his stories in book form called *Son of the Wolf*. The company described the book as "a vivid picture of the terrors of cold, darkness and starvation, the pleasures of human companionship in adverse circumstances and the sterling qualities which the rough battle with nature brings out."[3]

The book went on to be one of the best-selling works of the year. Success allowed Jack to do something poverty had prevented. He got married. By now, his relationship with Mabel had developed into a friendship. However, his friendship with Bess Maddern had developed into a relationship. Bess had been Jack's math tutor and her fiancé was a friend of his. When he was killed in the Spanish-American war, Jack attended the funeral. Bess and Jack began dating soon afterward and they were married on April 7, 1900. They would have two daughters. Joan was born in January, 1901 and Bess arrived in October the next year.

While Jack was married to his first wife Bess Maddern they had two daughters. Their daughters Bess (on the left) and Joan (on the right) are shown above in a photograph taken in 1913.

As his family grew, so did his fortunes. New York publisher S.S. McClure paid $100 a month for the right just to look at any short stories Jack wrote. McClure put them out in collections, and helped him sell them to magazines. Although the collections sold only moderately well, his novel *The Call of the Wild* would change his life. The novel told the story of Buck, an abused dog who returns to nature. It was a huge bestseller. It gave him international fame and would become his most popular book.

Most writers earn a royalty, a small percentage of the price for every book sold. Unfortunately, Jack had signed away his royalty rights for $2,000. Although his other novels would earn tens of thousands of dollars, that decision would cost him over $100,000—more than a million dollars in today's economy.

Suddenly, instead of finding rejection letters in the mail, Jack found checks. He was able to go on lecture tours. He spoke about socialism to female fans who came more for his rugged good looks than for his politics, and captains of industry who endured Jack's rants against capitalism in hopes of a good fish story. Newspapers hired Jack to report on conflicts like the Russo-Japanese War in 1904 and the Mexican Revolution a decade later. He wrote articles on social injustices in England and the tragic aftermath of the San Francisco Earthquake. Yet even as his wealth and fame grew, his problems seemed to grow as well.

FYInfo

SAN FRANCISCO EARTHQUAKE

San Francisco
Earthquake

The first wave of destruction arrived at 5:15 on the morning of April 18th, 1906. The earthquake was as loud as a freight train, rumbling in a wide swath across San Francisco. Smaller buildings fell down immediately; larger skyscrapers like the 12-story Call Building were twisted but remained standing. Modern analysts estimate that the quake measured 8.25 on the Richter scale, far worse than the 6.7 the one in 1989 registered.

Nearly a century ago, buildings were neither as strong nor as safe from fire as they are today. That night, Jack London wrote, "I walked through miles and miles of magnificent buildings and towering skyscrapers. Here was no fire. All was in perfect order. The police patrolled the streets. Every building had its watchman at the door. And yet it was doomed, all of it. There was no water. The dynamite was giving out. And at right angles two conflagrations were sweeping down upon it."[1]

It was the fire that did the most damage, and caused most of the estimated 450-700 deaths. Flames roared across the city as gas mains exploded. Elegant mansions and cheap hotels blazed equally. Watching as the Windsor Hotel caught fire, a man named Max Fast described how "there were three men on the roof, and it was impossible to get them down. Rather than see the crazed men fall in with the roof and be roasted alive the military officer directed his men to shoot them, which he did in the presence of 5,000 people."[2] Another eyewitness watched as a policeman tried to pull a trapped man from burning wreckage. As the flames reached him, the man begged the officer to shoot him. After taking the helpless man's name and address, the policeman shot him in the head.

The worst natural disaster in the history of the United States, by some accounts the San Francisco earthquake caused $3,000,000 in damage—a huge sum in those days.

Jack and Charmian Kittredge photographed with their dog. Charmian was fun-loving, flirtatious and just as wild as Jack was.

Chapter 5

THE HEIGHT OF TRIUMPH, THE DEPTH OF DESPAIR

Jack London was in his 30s and earning over $75,000 a year from writing and lecture tours. Although his annual income was equivalent to over one million dollars today, Jack was always in debt. Banks threatened to take his home and creditors promised legal actions. To Jack, holding onto money was difficult.

Jack's failed marriage to Bess Maddern would be yet another expense. In a letter to her he wrote, "Remember that when I asked you to marry me, and you accepted me, that it was there and then stated explicitly by me that I did not love you. You accepted me on that basis. Long afterwards, I found somebody whom I could love."[1]

This "somebody" was Charmian Kittredge. Jack had met her when he was writing for *The Overland Monthly*. She was a secretary there, the niece of his editor Roscoe Eames. That was in 1898. By July of

1903 they'd begun an affair. She was everything Bess was not. Bess was the woman he *thought* he should marry. She was sophisticated, educated and a good mother to his children.

Charmian was the woman Jack *wanted* to marry. She was fun-loving, flirtatious and just as wild as he was. In the early 1900s, women had few rights. They weren't even allowed to vote. But Jack treated Charmian as his equal. He called her his "mate woman."

In 1904, Bess sued for divorce. It became final late the following year. The next day he married Charmian during a stopover in Chicago in the midst of a lecture tour. The couple spent the following decade having adventures and spending his money.

They sailed to Tahiti and Hawaii on the *Snark*, a sailboat partially constructed by Charmian's Uncle Roscoe. He proved to be a much better editor than a boat builder. The boat seemed even worse than the one Jack made during his gold quest days. It was also far more expensive, costing a then extraordinary $30,000. Originally planned for a trip around the world, it never made a quarter of the distance.

When Jack wasn't sailing, he was buying land—tens of thousands of acres. Jack claimed in a letter to the *San Francisco Chronicle*, "I have been trying hard to get out of the writing game for many years. I have never liked to write and only took up the profession as the third and last choice of my life. It has been a miserable occupation, but I did it to make money and I made it."[2] While the statement was probably untrue, there's little question that Jack was a far better writer than rancher. The land he bought just gave him another thing in his life to pour money into as he bought the best plants and livestock.

Charmian stayed by Jack's side as he struggled with the ranches and the boat. She did everything she could to help. Having worked in publishing, she proved to be a talented editor for Jack's work. She was one of the few people whose criticisms he would tolerate. Unfortunately, as Jack approached his middle 30s, drinking began to consume him. He was afflicted by health problems, suffering everything from stomach pains to kidney ailments. The worst disease he fought was writer's block.

Quite suddenly, Jack had run out of ideas. In secret, he paid a struggling New York writer to come up with story ideas, paying seven dollars for each one he used. In a letter Jack warned him, "For heaven's sake, remember the ones I take, so that you won't make the mistake of writing them up yourself sometime."[3] The writer, Sinclair Lewis, became famous in 1920 with the publication of his novel *Main Street* and a decade later was the first American recipient of the Nobel Prize for Literature.

On November 22, 1916, Jack London died. He was 40 years old. The death certificate listed uremic poisoning, which related to his failing kidneys, as the cause. Although this would have killed him eventually, Jack sped his own death with morphine, a powerful drug he took to ease the pain. Two empty vials were found by his bed. Despite the death certificate, Jack London most likely committed suicide.

"To me the idea of death is sweet," Charmian remembered Jack telling her. "Think of it—to lie down and go into the dark, out of all the struggle and pain of living. To go to sleep and rest, always to be resting. When I come to die, I will be smiling at death."[4]

According to witnesses, there was a smile on Jack's face when he died.

FYInfo

THE RUSSIAN REVOLUTION

Karl Marx

In his book *The Iron Heel*, Jack London predicted a revolution of oppressed workers in the United States. That revolution never happened. There was, however, a revolution in Russia. Jack died a year too early to witness it. Had he lived, he might well have tried to report on the uprising.

For several centuries, Russia had been ruled by the tsars. Some of them were harsh and cruel. Most of the country's inhabitants were peasants, who lived in poverty. The seeds of change began to be planted in the late 19th century by the writings of Karl Marx and an increasing number of people who wanted to modernize the country and change the way it was governed. One of them was Vladimir Lenin, whose brother was executed for trying to assassinate Tsar Alexander III.

A peaceful demonstration in 1905 resulted in troops firing into the crowd, killing hundreds. The government enacted some reforms, but they didn't go far enough. With World War I going against the Russians and many people on the brink of starvation, Tsar Nicholas II was forced to give up his throne in March, 1917. A provisional government came to power, hoping to rule by democratic methods. In November, the communists under the leadership of Lenin overthrew the provisional government and seized power.

In Jack's socialist ideals, power was to be given to the people and their wealth would be shared equally. Instead, the communists ran a dictatorship as brutal as the Tsars' had been. Freedom of press, speech and religion did not exist, and those who opposed their rule were either killed or imprisoned. In 1922, Russia and 14 adjoining countries were linked together to form the Union of Soviet Socialist Republics, or the Soviet Union as it was also known. A secret police called the KGB watched over citizens and wielded extraordinary powers. The rule of communism lasted until the fall of the Soviet Union in 1991.

CHRONOLOGY

1876 Born John Griffith Chaney to Flora Wellman and William Chaney in San Francisco, California; mother marries John London

1881 Begins attending school in Alameda

1885 Family moves to farm in Livermore Valley

1886 Stepsister Eliza marries Capt. John Shepard

1887 Begins attending Cole Grammar School

1890 Drops out of school, begins working in a cannery

1891 Becomes an oyster pirate

1893 Joins sealing crew on the *Sophia Sutherland*; wins first prize in a writing contest

1894 Marches with Coxey's Industrial Army of the Unemployed in Washington, D.C.

1895 Enrolls at Oakland High School

1896 Leaves high school, is accepted at the University of California at Berkeley

1897 Travels to Klondike in search of gold

1898 Sells his first short story

1899 Sells "An Odyssey to the North" to *The Atlantic Monthly*

1900 Sells his first collection of short stories

1900 Marries Bess Maddern

1901 Daughter Joan is born

1902 Daughter Bess is born

1903 Publishes his first novel, *Call of the Wild*

1904 Covers the Russo-Japanese War; Bess sues for divorce

1905 Marries Charmian Kittredge

1907 Sets sail on the *Snark*

1913 Makes more money than any other author in the world

1916 Dies of kidney failure on his ranch in Glen Ellen, California

TIMELINE IN HISTORY

1835 Author Mark Twain is born.

1836 Mexican General Antonio Lopez de Santa Anna captures the Alamo and kills its defenders; he is defeated several weeks later and Texas becomes an independent republic.

1848 Gold is discovered at Sutter's Mill in California; it ignites the California Gold Rush the following year.

1850 California is admitted to the Union as the 31st state.

1859 Abolitionist John Brown's raid on Harper's Ferry, a federal arsenal in West Virginia, leads to his arrest and execution.

1865 The U.S. Civil War between northern and southern states comes to an end, resulting in the end of slavery and over 600,000 deaths.

1867 U.S. Secretary of State William Seward purchases Alaska from Russia for $7,000,000; the sale is widely ridiculed and Alaska becomes known as "Seward's Folly."

1870 Vladimir Lenin, founder of the Union of Soviet Socialist Republics (Soviet Union) is born.

1876 Alexander Graham Bell invents the telephone.

1878 Britain invades Afghanistan.

1886 The Statue of Liberty is erected in New York harbor.

1892 J.R.R. Tolkien, the author of *The Lord of the Rings*, is born.

1898 Hawaii is annexed to the United States as a territory.

1902 Writer John Steinbeck is born in California.

1905 In St. Petersburg, Russia, Tsar Nicholas II orders his army to fire on striking workers, killing hundreds.

1910 Author Mark Twain dies.

1912 The sinking of the British luxury liner *Titanic* kills more than 1,500 passengers and crew members.

1916 Mexican revolutionary leader Pancho Villa leads a raid into New Mexico, which kills 17 Americans.

1917 The Russian Revolution ends the reign of Tsar Nicholas II.

1922 The Union of Soviet Socialist Republics (Soviet Union) is formed under Russian leadership.

1924 Soviet leader Vladimir Lenin dies.

TIMELINE IN HISTORY (CONT'D)

1929 The stock market crash eliminates billions of dollars in wealth, leading to the Great Depression.

1933 Franklin Delano Roosevelt begins serving the first of his four terms as U.S. President.

1937 San Francisco's Golden Gate Bridge opens to traffic.

1941 A Japanese sneak attack on Pearl Harbor, Hawaii sends the United States into World War II.

1945 World War II ends.

1955 Walt Disney opens Disneyland in Anaheim, California.

1959 Alaska and Hawaii are admitted as the 49th and 50th states.

1960 John F. Kennedy defeats Richard Nixon for President in one of the closest elections in U.S. history.

1968 Civil Rights leader Martin Luther King, Jr. is assassinated at a motel in Memphis, Tennessee.

2004 Author Christopher Paul Curtis' third book, *Bucking the Sarge*, is published.

GLOSSARY

capitalism (KAP-it-uhl-izm)
economic system based on free market competition and private ownership of the means of production.

jute (JOOT)
a plant used to make sacking and rope.

panning (PAN-ning)
washing gravel or rocks in a pan searching for gold.

prospector (PROS-peck-tuhr)
someone who searches for gold.

sloop (SLUPE)
a type of sailboat, with one mast and one headsail.

socialism (SO-shul-izm)
economic system in which the producers of goods own the means to distribute them.

skiff (SKIFF)
a small, flat-bottomed boat.

FURTHER READING

For Young Adults

Claflin, Edward. *Jack London: Wilderness Writer*. New York: Kipling Press, 1987.

Dyer, Daniel. *Jack London: A Biography*. New York: Scholastic Press, 1997.

Streissguth, Thomas. *Jack London*. Minneapolis: Lerner Publications, 2001.

Works Consulted

Calder-Marshall, Arthur. *Lone Wolf: The Story of Jack London*. New York: Duell, Sloan and Pearce, 1961.

Franchere, Ruth. *Jack London: The Pursuit of a Dream*. New York: Crowell, 1962.

Kershaw, Alex. *Jack London: A Life*. New York: St. Martin's Press, 1997.

Kittredge, Charmian. *The Book of Jack London*. London: Harper Collins, 1992.

London, Jack. *John Barleycorn: Alcoholic Memoirs*. Cambridge, Massachusetts: Robert Bentley, Inc., 1964.

London, Jack. *Letters from Jack London*. Edited by King Hendricks and Irving Shepard. New York: The Odyssey Press, 1965.

London, Jack. *The Sea Wolf*. New York: Puffin Books, 1997.

London, Jack. *Smoke Bellew*. New York: Dover Publications, 1993.

Lundquist, James. *Jack London: Adventure, Ideas and Fiction*. New York: Ungar Publishing, 1987.

Stone, Irving. *Irving Stone's Jack London*. New York: Doubleday & Company, 1977.

Walker, Franklin. *Jack London and the Klondike*. San Marino, CA: Huntington Library, 1966.

On the Internet

Jack London Ranch Album: A Pictorial Biography
http://www.jacklondons.net/

Who Was Jack London
http://www.getyourwordsworth.com/WORDSWORTH-JackLondon.html

Jack London – His Life and Books (Jack London State Historic Park)
http://www.parks.sonoma.net/JLStory.html

Jack London International
http://www.jack-london.org/main_e.htm

Ina Coolbrith
http://www.cateweb.org/CA_Authors/Coolbrith.html

Friedrich Nietzsche
http://www.philosophypages.com/ph/niet.htm

The San Francisco Earthquake, 1906
www.eyewitnesstohistory.com/sfeq.htm

CHAPTER NOTES

Chapter 1
A Dangerous Journey
1. Franklin Walker, *Jack London and the Klondike* (San Marino, CA: Huntington Library, 1966), p. 87.
2. Alex Kershaw, *Jack London: A Life* (New York: St. Martin's Press, 1997), p. 63.

FYI: Gold Fever
1. Alex Kershaw, *Jack London: A Life* (New York: St. Martin's Press, 1997), p. 58.

Chapter 2 Hard Times
1. Jack London, *Letters from Jack London*, eds. King Hendricks and Irving Shepard (New York: The Odyssey Press, 1965), p. 4.
2. Jack London, *John Barleycorn: Alcoholic Memoirs* (Cambridge, Massachusetts: Robert Bentley, Inc., 1964), p. 42.
3. *Letters*, p. 4.
4. *John Barleycorn*, p. 53.
5. Ibid., p. 50.

Chapter 3
Workers of the World
1. Jack London, *The Sea Wolf* (New York: Puffin Books, 1997), p. 151.
2. Alex Kershaw, *Jack London: A Life* (New York: St. Martin's Press, 1997), p. 29.
3. Jack London, *John Barleycorn: Alcoholic Memoirs* (Cambridge, Massachusetts: Robert Bentley, Inc., 1964), p. 138.
4. Kershaw, p. 51.

Chapter 4
Literary Gold
1. Irving Stone, *Irving Stone's Jack London* (New York: Doubleday & Company, 1977), p. 542.
2. Jack London, *Letters from Jack London*, eds. King Hendricks and Irving Shepard (New York: The Odyssey Press, 1965), p. 19.
3. Alex Kershaw, *Jack London: A Life* (New York: St. Martin's Press, 1997), p. 89.

FYI: San Francisco Earthquake
1. Charmian Kittredge, *The Book of Jack London, Volume 2* (London: Harper Collins, 1992), p. 125.
2. The San Francisco Earthquake, 1906, www.eyewitnesstohistory.com/sfeq.htm

Chapter 5
The Height of Triumph, the Depth of Despair
1. Alex Kershaw, *Jack London: A Life* (New York: St. Martin's Press, 1997), p. 218.
2. Ibid., p. 216.
3. Jack London, *Letters from Jack London*, eds. King Hendricks and Irving Shepard (New York: The Odyssey Press, 1965), p. 485.
4. Charmian Kittredge, *The Book of Jack London, Volume 2* (London: Harper Collins, 1992), p. 75.

INDEX